Kyle Terry

Edition
Approved Paperback-Edition May 2023
Copyright © 2023 cub & calf,
Laurenson, Spilstr. 2, 14195 Berlin,
Germany
All rights reserved.
ISBN 9798393640101

Contents

A Primer to Your Fortune 4
    Who Are You? 4
    Why Did You Get this Book? 4
    A Little Bit of History 5
    What Should You Sell? 6
Step 1: 8
    Pick a Product 8
Step 2: 10
    Create Free Content 10
Step 3: 13
    Create Your Image 13
Step 4: 15
    Make Money 15
Is it a Scam? 20
    A Bit of Critical Thinking 20
    Pyramid Schemes and Multi-Level Marketing 23
    Other Scams To Be Aware Of 25
    Protect Yourself from Scammers 29
More Resources 31
    True Rags to Riches 31
    Words of Wisdom 32
    Links 33

A Primer to Your Fortune

Who Are You?

Quite simply: You are probably someone who wants to make money. You may be at the beginning of your career journey, full of ambition and drive after graduating from college, or you may have already spent several years in the corporate world and are now seeking new opportunities outside of the typical 9-5 grind. Maybe you faced challenges with formal education, or recently experienced job loss, which has led you to explore alternative ways of earning a living.

Maybe you are a stay-at-home parent and are looking for ways to contribute to your household income while managing your familial responsibilities. Or you could be a single parent in need of a job that provides flexibility to accommodate your unique circumstances.

Or are you simply broke, in debt, with no education and no prospect of ever making a lot of money, even when employed and working overtime?

Regardless of the reasons behind your quest for financial success, you are determined to find avenues to make money, and that's why you decided to invest in this book. You are eager to learn new strategies, gain valuable insights, and acquire the knowledge and tools necessary to achieve your financial goals.

Why Did You Get this Book?

On your quest to find a way to make money, and make it quick, you probably came across people online who claim to earn thousands, or even tens of thousands, of dollars per month while working only a few hours a day from the comfort of their own homes. You may have watched their videos, read their posts, and followed the links they provided to their products. However, despite your efforts, you may still find yourself unclear about what exactly they do and how they achieve such success. Am I correct?

Fret no more, as I am here to provide you with the answers you seek. In this book, I will not only reveal the secrets behind their methods but also provide you with a step-by-step guide on how to follow in their footsteps. However, ultimately, the decision on what path to take will be up to you.

A Little Bit of History

Many moons ago, there was a man called Clark Stanley who sold snake oil as a cure for everything and anything. "Rattlesnake King" Stanley was not the only one, of course, but his snake oil liniment was eventually examined and found to lack any snake oil and to be heavily overpriced for what it was (tallow, chili peppers, turpentine, and camphor).

"In popular culture, a particular kind of confidence trick is associated with the snake-oil salesman - the traveling salesman purports to be a doctor (with false credentials), selling fake medicines with boisterous marketing hype, often supported by pseudo-scientific evidence. To increase sales, an accomplice in the crowd (a shill) will often attest to the value of the product in an effort to provoke buying enthusiasm." (Wikipedia, "Snake Oil", last edited on 28 February 2023, Snake oil - Wikipedia)

After the snake-oil-salesman, other door-to-door salespeople emerged, selling various products such as vacuum cleaners, skin care products, insurances, magazine subscriptions, and medicinal remedies for your daily ailments, using persuasive techniques to sell products directly to consumers.

The once labor-intensive job of the travelling salesperson has shifted to the digital realm. It's not just the work of the salesperson that has moved online, but the products themselves have also transitioned to the digital world.

Yes, there are still companies or individuals selling physical products, such as vacuums or hand-made jewelry, but these are not the people you want to emulate if your goal is to become rich quickly. They are not selling the *dream* of instant wealth.

Instead, a new breed of online entrepreneurs has emerged, I like to call them the "rich-tokers" or "rich-tubers." These individuals leverage social media platforms to sell digital products, services, or knowledge that promise to help others achieve financial success. They may offer courses on e-commerce, affiliate marketing, personal finance, or sell e-books, digital templates, or software that claim to unlock the secrets of financial abundance.

The question then becomes: What do these "rich-tokers" and "rich-tubers" actually sell, and more importantly, what should YOU sell?

A reasonable advice for aspiring entrepreneurs would be to carefully consider the market demand, their own skills and expertise, and the authenticity and value of the products or services they plan to offer. It's important to focus on providing genuine value and solving real problems for customers, rather than simply chasing get-rich-quick schemes. Building a sustainable and successful online business requires strategic planning, hard work, and a commitment to delivering value to customers.

But this is not what the social media gurus do, so I will cut to the chase and let you in on their strategy.

What Should You Sell?

Anything you want, it doesn't really matter in the grand scheme of getting rich quick.

As an entrepreneur in the online world, your ultimate goal is to capture the attention and interest of customers and keep them coming back for more. Your success depends on convincing them that your product or service is the key to their dreams and aspirations, and that they can achieve their desired outcome by continuously engaging with your offerings. This continuous engagement translates into repeat purchases, with customers happily swiping their credit cards, and your bank account growing as a result. Savvy?

One of the intriguing aspects of these online business models is that you don't necessarily need personal experience or credentials, and you don't even have to sell physical products. Enthusiasm for the product or service you are promoting is preferred, but even that can be faked. You can tap into the shared dream of becoming wealthy that your potential customers likely have and use it to your advantage. After all, their dream of financial abundance is probably your dream as well.

If you're still confused about what exactly these get-rich-quick schemes entail and how you can attempt them, here's some good news. The next few pages will provide you with a step-by-step guide to replicate a scheme that promises to help you achieve your financial goals. Follow along as I walk you through the four easy-to-replicate steps that can potentially lead you to the riches you desire. Trust me, I've got you covered.

Step 1:
Pick a Product

But I don't have a product, I hear you say. Don't worry, that's not a problem at all. In fact, anything can work as a product. The key is to tap into people's dreams and insecurities. A great product is one that captures their imagination and promises to fulfill their desires or solve their problems. For example:

- Cryptocurrency
- Drop-shipping and sales
- Amazon FBA (Fulfillment by Amazon)
- Real estate
- Relationship tips
- Fitness and beauty
- Business strategies and marketing
- Writing reviews
- Writing fiction (no need to be an actual writer thanks to AI, see below)
- Selling digital products (PLR)
- ...

PLR: private label rights are digital products sold with a license to reuse.

What you should not do at this point is to attempt Bitcoin trading, drop-shipping, review writing, or digital template selling yourself, as these typically require a lot of effort to establish and rarely lead to substantial wealth, despite what some people may claim. Instead, you want to position yourself as the one who teaches others how to do these things.

You want to be the person who sells the shovels to the gold miner.

To create text (or later your online course content) and nice imagery, you can either hire someone for cheap, or go even cheaper and use one of the many artificial intelligence programs.

For example, ChatGPT can easily create written pieces tailored to your specific topic. Whether you're looking to craft short stories, poetry, self-help books, or educational non-fiction, ChatGPT can generate text pieces that you can combine and adjust with minimal effort. Just be aware that while ChatGPT can be a powerful tool, the texts it generates may not always make perfect sense. There may be instances where fiction and facts are mixed up, so it's essential to review and edit the output accordingly to ensure accuracy and coherence in the final content.

> AI: artificial intelligence programs are used to create texts and images.

Similarly, AI programs like Midjourney, Dall-E, or Lensa have gained popularity for generating images. These AI-powered tools can produce images that are remarkably close to reality, depending on the subject. From creating digital art to enhancing photographs, these AI programs offer creative possibilities for visual content generation.

While AI-powered content generation tools can be incredibly helpful and efficient, reviewing and editing the output generated by AI programs is crucial to ensure that the final content meets the desired standards and effectively communicates the intended message.

Step 2:
Create Free Content

Grab your phone or an old camera and film yourself telling people that you just made the rent for the month in just two hours of work.

If you are on social media, I'm sure you have seen people simply sitting in their cars shaking their heads in disbelief or sipping on a beverage looking bemused that no one else has figured out how easy it is to get rich.

The key to making a successful video is to keep it short and sweet. Five seconds on TikTok is enough to grab people's attention and leave them wanting more. Make sure to use eye-catching captions and visuals to showcase your success. You can also add a voiceover to your video to tell your viewers how much money you made or a few keywords about how you made your dream come true.

You might also have heard about the advice to create a 'funnel'.

> The **funnel**, sometimes also referred to as a marketing funnel or revenue funnel, describes a technique to get as many people as possible to see your product and then lead them to take more steps towards purchasing your product.

This 5-second clip on TikTok? This is already the edge of your funnel.

To maximize the potential of your TikTok clip and turn it into a profitable funnel, you need to create more content and post it frequently. The more content you create, the more chances you have of gaining new followers and potential customers. By consistently sharing your success stories and motivational messages, you can build a community of like-minded individuals who are interested in your message and your products.

Your content should be relevant to your niche and target audience, and you need to understand who your audience is and what they want. This should be easy, as their obvious connection is to become rich with ease, just like you.

At a later stage, you should expand your repertoire to longer videos, live streams, and even blog posts. By diversifying your content, you can keep your audience engaged and attract new followers who may prefer a different format. Also consider using multiple platforms, and if you have the time and energy, build your own website. Just keep in mind to not give away any actually useful information with your free content.

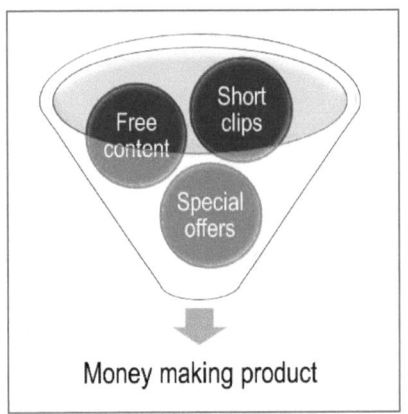

A funnel to guide customers to your money spinner.

Ultimately, the goal of your TikTok funnel is to convert your followers into paying customers. This means that you need to offer a product or service that solves a problem for your audience. By providing value and building trust with your followers, you can turn them into loyal customers who are happy to support your business. More about this in the next steps.

If you want to take your scheme to the next level and really sell the dream of luxury and wealth, consider borrowing or renting a fancy car or borrowing a friend's house for a video shoot. This will give you the appearance of a successful lifestyle, and people will be more likely to believe that you have achieved great wealth and success.

It is a well-known fact that seeing luxury products fuels the dream to become rich, and you definitely want your customers to become attached to your product which sells this dream.

But if you don't have access to luxury items or locations, don't worry. A little creativity can go a long way. For example, take advantage of free public spaces like parks or the beach and take pictures or videos that make it look like you're on an expensive vacation. Use props like sunglasses, a beach hat, or a cocktail to enhance the illusion.

You can also get creative with editing tools and filters to make your content look more professional and polished. There are plenty of apps available that allow you to add special effects, music, and text to your videos to make them more engaging and appealing.

And don't forget to keep an eye on what other successful influencers are doing. Pay attention to the types of content they're creating and the strategies they're using to engage their followers. Take note of the hashtags they're using and the times they're posting and use this information to refine your own approach.

Going to a public swimming pool? Take a picture of your legs in the crystal blue water and say you've just had the most amazing holiday.

Trying out a cheap face mask at home? Take a picture of your face close up and pretend you're at a luxury spa.

Got some nice flowers (preferably roses)? Spread the petals on a clean towel or bed and gush about how thoughtful that five-star hotel is that you are staying at for your birthday.

Remember, it's all about the image you present to your followers, so make sure everything looks professional and polished.

Step 3:
Create Your Image

Create some more free content to tell people about yourself, make them relate to you and show that you've been through struggles just like them.

Maybe you were broke after graduating college or never had the chance to pursue higher education. Perhaps you were afraid to fail, or you just wanted to spend more time with your family. Maybe you were burnt out from working a corporate 9-5 job and knew there had to be something more out there for you.

Whatever your backstory is (or whatever you invent as your backstory), turn on the camera and share it with your audience. Let them know that you are just like them and that if you can achieve your goals, so can they.

Dreams don't discriminate.

No matter your age, skin color, education, or nationality. No matter your circumstances, everyone can create a full income, just like you.

For further proof, add some testimonials that vouch for your success and the success you gave them. When it comes to testimonials, the more the better. Reach out to anyone you've ever helped, even if it was just giving them some advice or a quick tip. They might not have made a full income like you claim, but their words of praise and gratitude can still be powerful tools to convince others to buy into your scheme.

Just starting out and haven't help anyone yet? Ask your friends to give a spiel.

Remember to frame your message in a way that makes it seem like you're doing your potential customers a favor by offering them this opportunity.

Use phrases like "I want to help you achieve your dreams" or "I'm giving back by sharing my knowledge with others".

It's all about making them feel like they're part of an exclusive club that only a select few are privy to. Once they're hooked, you can start selling them your products or services with promises of quick and easy riches. Just remember to keep your claims vague and open-ended, so that you're never actually lying to your customers.

With some practice, you and your friends can become masters of the art of saying a lot without saying anything at all. Just be careful not to get caught up in your own hype, and always be transparent with your customers about what they're getting into and that it is up to them and the work they put in that tips the scale towards winning or losing. Not made any money? They were not working hard enough.

Last but not least, and personally, I'd rather you not do this, you will create free content that effectively discredits the friends and families of those who do not follow along or at least support them on their venture. They are just backward-thinking grudgers who envy your discovery of the holy grail. This is what most gurus and cult leaders do and why they are so effective.

Don't f#$@ with people's minds.

I don't like it because it can really mess with people's minds to alienate them from their naturally grown peer group, but for the sake of completion, here it is:

Tell them to expect people who won't believe or understand what you have discovered. They are just negative or jealous of your drive, not worth being in your life, and hold you back.

You want to isolate them from anyone who might try to speak rationally to them about making money. You want to rewire them and build a mindset that they need to spend money to make money.

Step 4:
Make Money

So far, you have created short free videos, articles, and social media posts to lure the customers down your funnel. They are hopefully hooked on the possibilities and the lifestyle that you showed them and click on your links, follow your profile, and post desperate questions to learn more about your secret.

The free content shouldn't have taken up much of your time, but you will have to keep it going. Remember, this is the edge of your funnel, and you want as many people as possible on its edge to slide down towards your actual money makers. But don't worry, after a while you can start reposting old content to ease your burden.

Now it gets a bit hairy, and you do need to put in some effort, but by now you should have mastered talking a lot without saying much.

To take your funnel to the next level, you need to create more comprehensive and detailed pieces of content that your audience can access for a fee. These could include online courses, workshops, and consulting services. You could also offer exclusive access to a membership site or a private community where your followers can connect with like-minded individuals and receive personalized support from you.

As you continue to produce content, keep in mind that you want to maintain a consistent brand voice and messaging across all platforms. This will help build trust with your audience and establish you as an authority in your niche.

Additionally, consider leveraging social media advertising to reach a wider audience and drive traffic to your funnel. By carefully targeting your ads, you can reach people who are most likely to be interested in your content and offerings.

But how do you learn what to teach if you want to create online courses or provide a consultancy service? Hopefully you have chosen something that you are already a little familiar with. If not, find some bloggers, YouTubers, or get a library book to replicate their content (just don't copy and paste as this is illegal and infringes upon the copyright of other creators). You could even use AI and have it create content for you.

The biggest secret is that all the information that you are going to sell to your customers is already freely available.

You can go to the length and create an actual course where you compile the most important bits of information in nicely digestible chunks. If you do that you are one of few and I applaud you, but you will have left the road of easy money.

Instead, just rattle of common knowledge and motivational talk like "think positive to attract positive energy" or "don't listen to the haters" or "define your target audience and tighten your keywords" …

Want to keep it going? It's as easy as this: Your funnel doesn't end with your online course. Your first course will be an introduction package where you tell them about your 5 or 10 step success plan that has worked so well for so many people.

Give enough details that your customers are satisfied but withhold detailed information which you promise to give in your advanced course.

To truly make money, you need to make your customers feel like they are part of an exclusive club. Offer them a VIP membership or a monthly subscription service that promises even more exclusive content and access to "insider" information. This can be as simple as a monthly newsletter or a private Facebook group where they can connect with other like-minded individuals.

The key is to make them feel like they are getting something that no one else can have access to.

Here are some general steps for your introductory course that can be applied to almost any topic:

> 1. Find/make the right product.
> 2. Research the market.
> 3. Decide on a product.
> 4. Create a website.
> 5. Define your target audience.
> 6. Create online ads.
> 7. ...

You can expand your online course to a premium package where you offer even more valuable information like getting the most out of SEO (search engine optimization), finding the best keywords to improve your ads, or introducing many more (no-name) platforms to run ads/find products/analyze ad performance/... Simply check what your customers ask in their posts or direct messages and then offer your answers to a premium price.

Do not directly respond to anyone's questions, but create more content and refer them to your other videos, articles, blog posts, or courses. Keep them in a loop where they only consume your content, as here is another psychological trick: the more often your customers see and listen to you, the more familiar you become, which in turn creates trust in you.

As soon as you have your course ready, make sure that every piece of free content includes a link to it, so that people can follow the breadcrumbs leading them down your funnel to your end goal.

The advanced course tackles each of these steps individually and answers some of your customer's questions, which might be:

- Where do I buy my products?
- Which platforms are best to create a website?
- Where do I find my target audience?
- How much should I spend on ads?
- How to create ads for different platforms (Google, Facebook,...)
- Find the best keywords and game the SEO algorithm.
- How often, at what time, and with which tags should you post on social media
- ...

Once you have your online courses recorded and ready, start to diversify. By now, you should be familiar enough with your topic that you can offer in-person consultations where people can call or Zoom with you for 30 minutes or an hour to get private access to your knowledge. Of course, you will charge even more for this privilege.

Pretending to run a sale or a limited-time offer also puts the gun to people's head, and if they are already contemplating buying your course, this is now the final straw for them to scramble, giving you their money.

Of course, you don't have to lower your price for real, even though this would be the ethical thing to do. Just like brick-and-mortar shops run their sales, increase your price first before you take off 20 or 30% or even 50%, just to arrive at the same price that you were already charging. Some sellers have their products constantly on sale.

And finally, you can slap your information together into a book and sell it without any costs on Amazon. I do not recommend this as you cannot sell books for a high enough price without losing your online course customers, but it can be an additional piece in your funnel to tap into a larger market.

Should you get to the point where you have a following, create some merchandise. Cups or T-shirts are easy to offer with print-on-demand sites like Redbubble or through your very own shop on Shopify. Only at the point of having a hooked fan base should you go down this route; otherwise, it is only a topic that you should teach about.

And finally, once you think you have exhausted one topic, start the whole process again with a different one. Upsell your customers on related products or services. For example, if you sell an online course on how to make money through social media marketing, you could also offer them a social media management service or a consultation package. By constantly offering them new opportunities to invest in their success, you can keep the money rolling in and continue to grow your business.

A word of advice to keep disappointed customers from snitching on you: make sure to let your customers know that their success is still up to them. You only give them the tools, but they will have to put in the work. If they are not succeeding, then it is their own fault. They may not work hard enough, don't follow all your advice, drop out too early, or simply are not in the right mindset and don't believe in their own success enough. The last argument is a silver bullet as it can neither be proven nor counterproven, something that is often used by cult leaders to trap their followers and make them feel guilty about their own unworthiness.

Is it a Scam?

A Bit of Critical Thinking

What you see is not what you get, at least with most online courses that promise a quick profit.

If it sounds too good to be true, it probably is.

Just like the content creators, you can find most information that you need for free. That is not to say that all online courses are bad and not worth your while or money, but the age old saying "if it sounds too good to be true, it probably is" should be on the top of your mind.

There is no such thing as a getting-rich-quick scheme. That is just someone else getting rich off you. Anything worthwhile takes time and effort, and there are no shortcuts to success. It is up to you to put in the time, money, and effort necessary to achieve your goals.

Most if not all ways to make money only let you choose one or a maximum of two out of three things. Those three things are: time, money, and effort.

If you want to make money quickly and without much effort, be prepared to spend a lot of money. On the other hand, if you want to save money and not spend much, you will need to put in a lot of time and effort. And if you want to save time and not put in much effort, you will need to spend a lot of money.

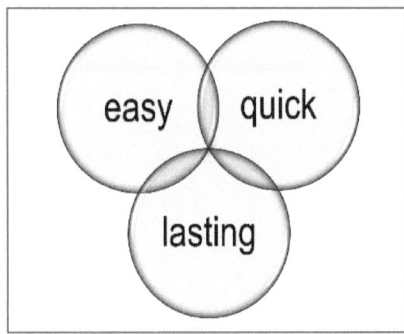

You only get to pick two at most to make money.

Quick and easy:

Invest in crypto currency or pursue any of the latest fads but be aware that your riches most likely won't last and your quick and easy money won't be enough to retire or live a plush life for long.

Easy and lasting:

Invest in secure stocks or shares and in 30+ years your money will have multiplied without you having had to lift a finger (check out my new book on investing at the stock market: The Private Investor).

Lasting (but neither quick nor easy):

Provide quality work and keep your customers happy. The best of all options, but it won't be easy, and you do have to put in the work. The quick part is also unlikely, as you probably will have to educate yourself in some form or another (remember, there are great free resources out there) and establish yourself as a trustworthy businessperson.

Here are some more pointers for you to decide whether an online course or offer for consultancy is worth it:

- Are the prices justifiable?
  - Does the person offering the course have actual and verifiable credentials? Keep in mind that it is easy to set up websites and even LinkedIn profiles with a fake work history and experiences. A dead giveaway is if all evidence was created by the content creator themself.
  - Will you have to work for months to make the money back?
- Are the promised outcomes realistic?
  - Promising six-figure salaries or making rent money within a couple of hours on the back of an online course is ludicrous unless you are already the CEO of a multimillion-dollar company, in which case you surely don't need this course. Earning a couple of hundred-dollar pocket money? That's more realistic for the little work that these courses promise.
- Do you encounter phrases like: "I can't believe that not more people have figured this out!", "You don't need experience to make six figures." "Start earning a passive income without any risk and no skill involved." "It's essentially free today (use your credit card or PayPal credit)", "After this course, you'll want to quit your job"? ...
  - That's psychology wash to trap you in the dream and stop you from listening to any real-world advice.

Pyramid Schemes and Multi-Level Marketing

A pyramid scheme is started by an entrepreneurial scammer who promises to invest your money or start a company that will give great returns. Next, they tell you that you can get even more money back if you recruit other people.

In a pyramid scheme, early investors recruit others into the scheme, who in turn recruit others, and so on, forming a pyramid-shaped structure. The only way for participants to make money is by recruiting new members, and eventually, the number of new members needed to sustain the scheme exceeds the available population, causing the pyramid to collapse.

Your hard-earned money filters up, the entrepreneurial scammer gets some free cash to play with, but you will never ever see your money returned let alone with interest.

As a result, only the top members of the pyramid make significant profits, while the vast majority of participants lose their money.

This practice is rightfully illegal in most countries.

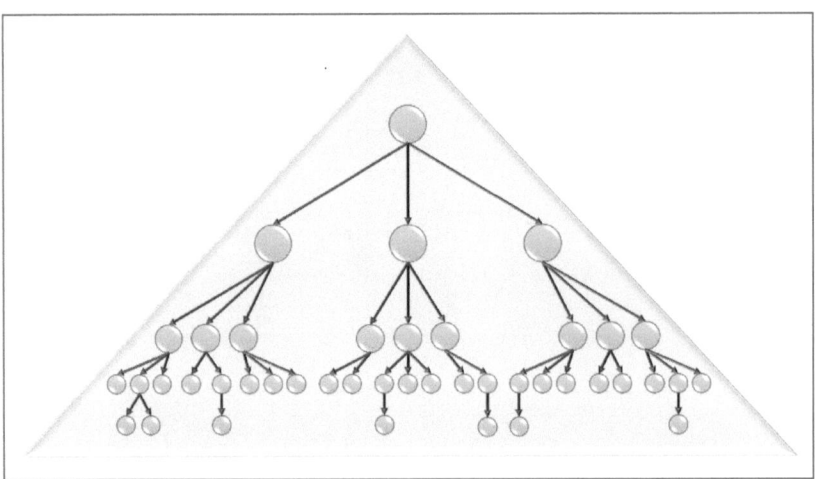

Pyramid scheme: Only the top makes money, the majority on the bottom loses out.

Multi-level marketing (MLM) is like a pyramid scheme, with the only difference being that they have an actual product that you are supposed to sell. Most of the time, this product is like the snake-oil of yore, with subpar quality and dubious benefits.

> Pyramid schemes are often disguised as MLMs.

Again, with every person you recruit, you will get a percentage of their sales which increases your own income from the scheme. If the emphasis is on the recruiting side, then this MLM qualifies as a pyramid scheme, which is why MLM programs make sure to tell you how awesome their product is.

Personally, I think, if their products were really so great, they wouldn't rely on untrained, unqualified people for their sales team (yes, I know they often offer training, but really is this not another way of trapping you in their scheme?).

Because these schemes proclaim that the main income source is selling the product and not from recruiting more sellers, they are not illegal. But just like a pyramid scheme it is more likely that you invest more money (to buy stocks and go on training courses) than you will ever see in return.

Pyramid schemes are often disguised as multi-level marketing (MLM) companies, which is why it can be difficult to distinguish between the two. MLM companies do allow you to earn money by recruiting other people, but the main difference is that they have a legitimate product or service that they are selling. In a pyramid scheme, there is no real product or service being sold, and the only way to make money is by recruiting more people into the scheme.

Unfortunately, pyramid schemes continue to exist because scammers are always finding new ways to disguise them. They might claim to be selling a revolutionary new product or service, or they might use complex financial jargon to make the scheme seem more legitimate. It's important to always do your research and be wary of any "opportunities" that promise quick and easy money. Remember, if something sounds too good to be true, it probably is.

With both MLM and pyramid schemes, the only persons to ever make money are the founders or at best the first generation to buy into these schemes. By the time you and I hear from and get invited to them, the money train has long left.

So, either start your own MLM with a carefully chosen product or run away from them. Do not even consider buying any stock of this latest health drink, this super reusable packaging, this energy pendant, or rejuvenating face cream.

At the most, try out some free samples and see whether you like them for your own, personal, not-for-profit use, but be prepared to lose a friend when you tell them that you won't become another snowball in their fight to get rich quick.

Other Scams To Be Aware Of

I do not condone online courses that give you the foundation to build an income. In fact, I love online courses and would recommend the good ones to anyone. There are so many out there, for free and on various topics, that there should really be no one having to pay to get the information they need. Many universities even put their lectures online for the general public to enjoy and expand their horizons. The issue comes in when you are asked to pay money, especially if it is amounts that you cannot easily forget about and move on.

Here are some examples of scams to be wary of:

Work-From-Home Scams: These scams promise the opportunity to earn money from home with little effort, often by promoting fake business opportunities, envelope stuffing, or online jobs that require upfront fees. In reality, you may end up losing money or personal information.

Fake Business Opportunities: Scammers may promote fake business opportunities that promise the chance to earn money from home by investing in a business or franchise. They may require upfront fees for training materials, software, or other resources, but in reality, the promised business does not exist or is not profitable.

Envelope Stuffing Scams: These scams claim that you can earn money by stuffing envelopes at home. However, you are often required to pay for a startup kit or materials, and the work is usually not legitimate or does not pay as promised.

Online Jobs Scams: Scammers may pose as legitimate employers offering work-from-home jobs, such as data entry, customer service, or virtual assistance, but require upfront fees for training, equipment, or other expenses. In reality, you may never receive any work or payment for their services.

Phishing Scams: Phishing scams involve fraudsters posing as legitimate organizations, such as banks, online payment platforms, or government agencies, to trick you into revealing your personal and financial information. This information is then used for identity theft or financial fraud.

Investment Scams: Investment scams lure you with promises of high returns on investments, but in reality, they are fraudulent schemes that aim to steal money from unsuspecting victims. Examples include Ponzi schemes, where returns are paid to earlier investors using funds from new investors, and fake investment opportunities that promise guaranteed returns with little or no risk.

Online Auction and Marketplace Scams: These scams involve fraudulent sellers on online auction or marketplace platforms who do not deliver the products as promised or sell counterfeit goods. Buyers may lose money and receive fake or subpar products.

Romance Scams: Romance scams involve fraudsters creating fake online profiles on dating websites or social media, building a relationship with victims, and then asking for money under false pretenses, such as medical emergencies or travel expenses.

Tech Support Scams: Tech support scams involve scammers pretending to be from well-known tech companies, claiming that your computer has a virus or technical issue and asking for remote access or payment for fake services.

Lottery or Sweepstakes Scams: These scams let you know that you have won a lottery or sweepstakes but require you to pay fees or taxes upfront to claim your prize. In reality, there is no prize, and victims lose their money.

Fake Charities or Donation Scams: These scams involve fake charities or donation requests, often in response to natural disasters or other tragic events, where scammers collect money from bona fide Samaritans with no intention of using it for charitable purposes.

Payment Processing Scams: These scams try to recruit you as payment processors, where you are asked to receive payments from customers, process them through your personal bank accounts, and then transfer the funds to another account, often overseas. However, the payments are usually from illegal activities, and victims may unknowingly become involved in money laundering or other illegal activities.

Mystery Shopping Scams: Scammers may claim that you can make money by becoming a mystery shopper, where you evaluate the quality of services or products at retail stores or restaurants. You are required to pay for a list of opportunities or for access to assignments, but in reality, the assignments are often fake or do not pay as promised.

Reshipping Scams: These scams ask you to receive and repackage goods, which are often obtained through fraudulent means, and then ship them to another address, usually overseas. Victims may unknowingly become involved in illegal activities and may not receive payment as promised.

Fake Influencer/Model/Agent Scams: Scammers create fake accounts pretending to be influencers, models, or talent agents and reach out with promises of modeling gigs, brand collaborations, or representation. They may ask for upfront fees, personal information, or even explicit content, but in reality, there are no real opportunities, and victims may end up losing money, compromising their privacy, or being exploited.

Fake Giveaway Scams: Scammers create fake accounts that mimic popular influencers or brands and run fake giveaways. They may ask participants to follow, like, share, or comment on their posts, and promise lucrative prizes. However, the winners are never actually chosen, and scammers may use this tactic to gain followers, engagement, or personal information for nefarious purposes.

Fake Online Stores/Products Scams: Scammers create fake online stores or product pages on Instagram and other social media platforms, offering enticing deals on products or services. They may ask for payment upfront but never deliver the products, or send counterfeit or low-quality items. Victims may end up losing their money or receiving inferior products.

It's important to be cautious and thoroughly research any work-from-home opportunity before investing money or sharing personal information. Legitimate work-from-home opportunities should not require upfront fees for training or materials, and it's important to verify the legitimacy of the opportunity with trusted sources. Report any suspected work-from-home scams to the relevant authorities to help protect others from falling victim to these fraudulent schemes.

Protect Yourself from Scammers

Remember, scammers are constantly evolving their tactics, and it's important to be vigilant and cautious when coming across someone who tells you that you can make easy money, or a lot of it in very little time. Always verify the legitimacy of accounts, do your research, protect your personal information, and trust your instincts to avoid falling victim to scams.

Verify Accounts: Always verify the legitimacy of an account before engaging with it or providing any personal information. Look for verified badges, check the account's history, followers, and engagement, and do not trust accounts that seem suspicious or have little to no activity. Accounts can buy followers and even likes or generic comments, but true engagement shows as organic and human-sounding comments on their posts.

Be Cautious of Unsolicited Messages: Be wary of unsolicited messages, especially those that ask for personal information, payment, or explicit content. Legitimate influencers, brands, or businesses typically do not reach out to individuals with unsolicited offers.

Do Your Research: Research any investment opportunities, online stores, or products before making any payment or providing personal information. Look for reviews, testimonials, or feedback from trusted sources. The emphasize is on "trusted" as you should have learned in Step 3 that it is a vital step to create fake testimonials for scammers.

Protect Your Personal Information: Be cautious about sharing personal information, passwords, or financial details on or through social media platforms. Legitimate companies or individuals do not ask for sensitive information through direct messages.

Trust Your Instincts: If something seems too good to be true or feels suspicious, trust your instincts, and proceed with caution. Do not engage with accounts or individuals that raise red flags.

Report Suspicious Accounts: If you come across suspicious accounts or suspect any online scams, report them to the respective platform or relevant authorities to help protect others from falling victim to similar scams.

More Resources

True Rags to Riches

You don't have to wait until you're of age, broke, or burnt out to turn your life around. Similarly, you don't have to hold yourself back because you think you are beyond your prime. There are plenty of stories where people didn't take "no" for an answer, and if children can start a business (with the help of legal guardianship), so can you.

Take Hart Main, who created manly scented candles after teasing his sister with them.

Kamaria Warren and her mom invented brown girl stationery because they couldn't find any while shopping for birthday invitations (it's worth noting that her mother was already a graphic designer).

Moziah Bridges taught himself how to sew to have a suitable bowtie and eventually started his business with handmade men's ties and bows.

There are thousands of creatives who found their niches selling homemade products on platforms like Etsy, Redbubble, and Amazon Merch. Some even reach a point where they require expanding and hiring staff to help with production and sales.

"But I don't have any talent, and I can't come up with a unique product," you say? Well, do you know about the Oodie? It's a wearable blanket that blew up in Australia and made then 24-year-old Dave Fogarty a millionaire within a year. But before he hit gold with the Oodie (a product he sourced through manufacturers found on AliExpress), he went through years of making money and losing it with various business ideas.

Most importantly, though, these years were his apprenticeship of sorts, teaching him how to test products, market them, and create sales and storage infrastructure. By the time he decided on the Oodie, he was a well-versed business entrepreneur who could act fast. Remember, success does not come overnight, but with persistence and determination, you too can achieve your goals.

Words of Wisdom

Don't believe that you can easily recreate Dave Fogarty's success by starting a drop-shipping business just because someone on social media says so. There are plenty of other people out there who are also telling you, for free, why drop-shipping is a bad idea. And they are not just grudgers who want to hold you back. Take their advice and adjust your course of action accordingly.

You see, Dave Fogarty's story is not a get-rich-quick story. It is a story of trial and error, tenacity, and probably a bit of luck that trumped a university degree. The best part is that Dave talks about his success and approach on his YouTube channel for free.

You can learn about business models, sales, marketing, insurance, and taxes online for free. Find out how to approach funders, create ad campaigns, film and edit videos, tighten your keywords, and get good energy mantras online for free.

Just like the person who is trying to sell their course has found all their information somewhere, you can do it too. Of course, you can also become one of them and make money selling courses to the desperate. In that case, go back to Step 1 of this book and follow through. I won't judge you, but expect that it won't be as easy, quick, or even as lasting as you might think it will be.

Links

I compiled a list of websites and YouTube channels to get you started, either on your journey to make some money or to confirm whether something is a scam.

You will see that I reference Reddit a lot as it gives positive and negative insights into almost every topic and I highly recommend checking out this well of knowledge.

This is by no means all the resources and I encourage you to do your own research and find what suits your goal.

Drop-shipping and Retail:
https://www.shopify.com/
https://www.shopify.com/dropshipping
https://apps.shopify.com/oberlo
https://www.etsy.com/
https://www.oberlo.com/blog/etsy-dropshipping
https://www.reddit.com/r/dropshipping/
https://merch.amazon.com/
https://www.reddit.com/r/AmazonMerch/comments/ruu07v/is_merch_still_a_good_and_viable_opportunity/
https://sell.amazon.com/fulfillment-by-amazon
https://www.reddit.com/r/Entrepreneur/comments/sqfjc1/do_amazon_fba_sellers_actually_make_money/
https://www.aliexpress.com
https://www.alibaba.com/
https://www.redbubble.com/

Cryptocurrency and Investing
https://www.reddit.com/r/CryptoCurrency/
https://www.investopedia.com/
https://www.investing.com/
https://www.marketwatch.com/

https://investor.vanguard.com/home

Real Estate
https://www.apartmenttherapy.com/
https://www.nerdwallet.com/
https://www.investopedia.com/

Relationships
https://www.reddit.com/r/relationship_advice/
https://www.psychologytoday.com/us
https://www.marriage.com/

Beauty Products
https://www.nytimes.com/guides/tmagazine/skincare-routine
https://www.goodhousekeeping.com/

Digital Content and PLR
https://www.fiverr.com/
https://www.midjourney.com/home/
https://openai.com/blog/chatgpt
https://www.canva.com/
https://kdp.amazon.com/

Advertising and Marketing
https://ads.google.com/home/
https://www.facebook.com/business/ads
https://www.redditforbusiness.com/
https://www.wordstream.com/blog/ws/2022/07/18/social-media-advertising
https://www.bigcommerce.com/articles/omnichannel-retail/social-media-advertising/

YouTube
@JamesJani

@Coffeezilla
@DavieFogarty
@thisdayinai
@leonjhendrix
@forbes

Other books by the author:

www.ingramcontent.com/pod-product-compliance
Lightning Source LLC
Chambersburg PA
CBHW041943240526
45473CB00033B/492